WHAT GOES ON INSIDE YOUR BRAIN?

MEMORY AND YOUR BRAIN

ROBYN HARDYMAN

Gareth Stevens
PUBLISHING

Please visit our website, **www.garethstevens.com**.
For a free color catalog of all our high-quality books,
call toll free 1-800-542-2595 or fax 1-877-542-2596.

Cataloging-in-Publication Data
Names: Hardyman, Robyn.
Title: Memory and your brain / Robyn Hardyman.
Description: New York : Gareth Stevens Publishing, 2019. | Series: What goes on inside
your brain? | Includes glossary and index.
Identifiers: ISBN 9781538235638 (pbk.) | ISBN 9781538235645 (library bound)
Subjects: LCSH: Memory--Juvenile literature. | Brain--Juvenile literature.
Classification: LCC BF371.H378 2019 | DDC 153.1'2--dc23

First Edition

Published in 2019 by
Gareth Stevens Publishing
111 East 14th Street, Suite 349
New York, NY 10003

© 2019 Gareth Stevens Publishing

Produced by Calcium
Editors: Sarah Eason and Claudia Martin
Designers: Paul Myerscough and Jeni Child

Photo credits: Cover: Shutterstock/Tyler Olson. Inside: Shutterstock: Africa Studio: p.10tc;
Aleks vF: p.10bl; Amero: p.10tl; Ampyang: p.3, p.14; Anurake Singto-On: p.23; Artem
Oleshko: p.21; Bojan Milinkov: p.35; Carla Van Wagoner: p.33; Carlos Aranguiz: p.11cr;
Caron Watson: p.30; chombosan: p.45; Cliparea/Custom Media: p.25r; Cookie Studio: p.1;
David Tadevosian: p.16; Decade3D/Anatomy Online: p.25l; DiversityStudio: p.29; Docent:
p.37; GaudiLab: p.9; Gines Romero: p.7; happydancing: p.39; Igordabari: p.12; Ivanko80:
p.18; Jacob Lund p.26; Jorge Salcedo: p.24; Joseph Sohm: p.27; Maks Narodenko: p.10br;
Monkey Business Images: p.15, p.17, p.32, p.44; Nick Nick: p.10bc; nobeastsofierce:
p.6; Oleksandr Lytvynenko: p.11tr; Ollyy: p.31; pathdoc: p.40; Photographee.eu: p.34;
Ray49: p.11c; Rocketclips, Inc.: p.42; Sebastian Kaulitzki: p.4, p.43; Sergey Nivens: p.36;
sfam Photo: p.28; Stockforlife: p.10tr; Studio Romantic: p.8; Suzanne Tucker: p.20; Syda
Productions: p.19; 2xSamara.com: p.38; Victoria Rak: p.22; Vitaliy 73: p.11tr; WaitForLight:
p.5; US National Institute on Aging, Alzheimer's Disease Education and Referral Center:
p.41.

Printed in the United States of America

CPSIA compliance information: Batch #CW19GS
For further information contact Gareth Stevens, New York, New York at 1-800-542-2595.

CONTENTS

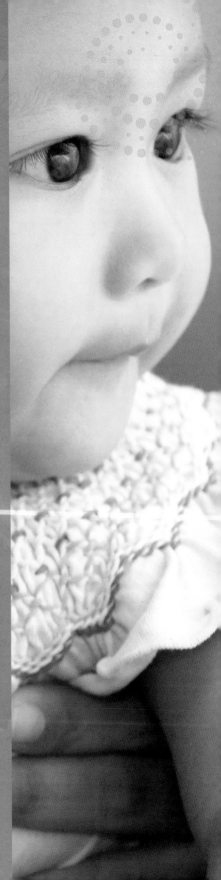

CHAPTER 1

THE HUMAN BRAIN

Parietal lobe

Frontal lobe

Temporal lobe

The human brain is the most powerful—and mysterious—object on the planet. You use your brain to do everything: to move, to think, to speak, to read. Yet your brain also contains all your "inner life"—your feeling and your memories. Our memories are one of the key things that make us human. Memory is one of the most mysterious superpowers that our brains perform every day.

The frontal lobe is behind your forehead. The parietal lobe is on the top of your head, and the temporal lobes are at the sides. At the back is the occipital lobe.

Scientists have come a long way in recent decades in understanding how the brain works, but there is still a lot to discover. So what do we know? We know that the brain is like the body's supercomputer, controlling everything that it does. It is about the size of your two fists put together, weighs about 3 pounds (1.4 kg), and its surface is gray and deeply wrinkled. It is divided into two equal halves, called the right and left hemispheres. The wrinkled surface layer is called the cerebral cortex. This is where most of the thinking happens, as well as movement, language, and memory.

The Parts of the Brain

Each half of the brain is divided into four main regions, called lobes. There is a lot of crossover between where different processes happen, but the frontal lobe is associated with reasoning and planning. The parietal lobe is associated with processing sensory information. The occipital lobe is associated with vision. Along with other areas, the temporal lobe is associated with memory, recognition of sounds, and speech. Deep inside the brain, below the lobes, are other structures that control our most basic actions. The cerebellum controls the working of our muscles, and the brain stem controls our heartbeat and breathing.

INSIDE YOUR BRAIN

The surface of the cerebral cortex is deeply creased so that a large surface area can fit inside the skull. The brains of less intelligent animals have a less wrinkled cortex. Your brain has hundreds of thousands of times more processing power than the most advanced computer, which means it needs an amazing amount of energy. In fact, it uses 20 percent of your energy!

Our ability to learn and remember information and skills has made us the most intelligent—and powerful—species on the planet.

What Is Memory?

Your memory tells you everything about the world, everything you know, and everything you have ever done. You know how to read, how to use a phone, and how to find your way to school because of your memory. You also know you had that great vacation with your grandparents, or that amazing time with your friends, or that special moment with your mom, because of your memory. How are all these extraordinary skills and experiences stored in our brains?

To understand it, we have to get close up inside the brain, to see what it's made of in detail. Your brain is made of cells, like every other part of you. Brain cells are called nerve cells, or neurons, and they look different from other cells. Each one has long tentacles, which it uses to connect to lots of other neurons. There are about 100 billion neurons in your brain, each with up to 10,000 connections, and together they form an incredible network—like the most advanced information superhighway you can imagine.

Neurons send messages to each other as electrical signals, at speeds of up to 250 miles per hour (400 km/h). Trillions of signals are being sent around your brain every second. As we grow and learn, the connections between neurons grow too, making the network more complex. Many new connections are made, and old ones are strengthened by being used over and over. This is how memory works. As we learn and practice a skill, the pathway in the network that allows us to do that gets stronger, until

Neuron

Axon

Dendrite

Neurons have one extra-long tentacle, called the axon, that sends signals out. They also have lots of smaller ones, called dendrites, which receive incoming signals.

we can perform that skill easily. When we need to use that skill again, we remember how to do it. It may be something simple such as tying a shoelace, or more complex such as riding a bike.

Learning a complex skill involves creating and strengthening many networks of neurons.

The part of the brain that allows us to think is the cerebral cortex, the outside layer. It sends information to other parts of the brain, to be stored. Scientists think that we store memories in several different areas of the brain, depending on what kind of memories they are, and what we need them for.

INSIDE YOUR BRAIN

The brain gives us our awareness, or our sense of self, which we call consciousness. It's difficult to define consciousness. It includes our awareness of the world around us, and also the thoughts we have inside our head. The real mystery comes when we try to understand consciousness. We are using our brain to try to understand our brain!

CHAPTER 2

SHORT-TERM MEMORY

The brain is not only incredibly powerful, but organized, too. It needs to be, because all the time we are taking in an awesome amount of information from all around us, and performing complex tasks that less intelligent creatures could never do. The brain has to be great at sorting out what is more or less important for us to remember. Sometimes we only need to retain information for a short time.

Remembering how to swim uses long-term memory, but remembering to pack your goggles uses short-term memory.

One morning, you wake up and remember you are going swimming, so you must find your gear. Then, when you are in the water, you must remember how to swim! There are two different types of memory at work here. When we need to remember things only for a short while, they are stored in our short-term memory. We do not need to use up valuable, long-term storage capacity on them. So when you remember you need to take your swimming gear with you, you do not need that memory after you have left the house with the right things. The memory of how to swim, however, is long-term memory. Imagine remembering every tiny thing you notice all the time. You would very quickly get brain overload! Your brain selects the things you need to remember, and decides how long you need to know them for.

Working Memory

Short-term memory allows you to hold and process information at the same time. So, for example, as you read this sentence you need to hold the beginning of it in your short-term memory while you read to the end of it, so that you can understand it. This is also called your working memory. Your mom tells you a telephone number and asks you to dial it for her. You remember that number only for as long as it takes you to dial. Within probably less than a minute, the memory is gone.

INSIDE YOUR BRAIN

Scientists think that the area of the brain that deals with short-term memory is in the prefrontal lobe of the cortex, at the front of our head. Your short-term memory is incredibly useful but it is much, much smaller than your long-term memory. We find it difficult to remember numbers with more than six or seven digits, for example.

When you remember a phone number for as long as it takes to use the keypad, you are using your working memory.

Look at these 10 objects for 30 seconds, then close the book. Wait for 1 minute, then see how many of the objects you can remember. Check back to see how you did.

Sensory Memory

The shortest kind of memory we have is called sensory memory. These are memories delivered by our senses, such as sight and hearing. For example, we can catch just a glimpse of something for less than a second, and still have a memory of what it looked like. This happens automatically—we do not choose to remember it. The signals from our eyes reach our brain and get stored, just for a tiny moment. This sensory memory can be a powerful tool for people who want to influence our thinking. Advertisers sometimes try to use it to persuade us to buy products. They flash images and messages very quickly on the television screen. We are not really aware of having seen them, but they have reached our sensory memory, and they just might get transferred to a longer-term memory store. Mostly, though, these memories fade almost immediately.

Retaining Memory

Although we cannot hold complex information in our short-term memory, scientists have discovered some factors that make it easier for us to retain it. For example, if we are learning a list of words, we will find it easier if they sound similar. So a list that goes "cat, hat, mat, that" is much easier to remember than "cat, dog, each, why." It is also easier if the words' subjects are related, such as all being animals or sports, and if they are short, with only one syllable. English speakers can remember up to seven digits in a sequence, but Chinese speakers can typically hold 10. Their memories are not better, but all Chinese number words have only one syllable.

SPEAK YOUR MIND

Scientists think that our short-term memory may be affected by our surroundings. Two groups of people were tested on their working memory skills, one group after a walk in a quiet park, the other after a walk through a busy city. The people who had walked in the city scored lower in the tests. How do you think the busy streets could have affected their attention and their short-term memory? Give reasons for your answer.

Boost Your Memory

If short-term memories are often forgotten within a few minutes, what can we do to improve that? Sometimes it would be useful to be able to hold on to things in our working memory for a bit longer.

One way to boost your short-term memory is to somehow shorten, or condense, the items you are trying to remember. So, for example, instead of trying to memorize the eight numbers, 5, 1, 5, 2, 6, 3, 7, and 0, you can condense them down to 51 52 63 70. It is easier to remember these four items than eight. This process is called chunking, because you are separating the numbers into chunks.

Another technique to help you remember things is to link each item to another piece of information. This is called mnemonics. Linking a number or a letter to something else really does make it easier to remember. For example, "mnemonic" is quite a difficult word to spell. To remember how to do it, you could invent a sentence using the letters, such as:

This is the number pi. Remembering a long string of digits such as this requires very special memory skills.

$\pi = 3.141592$

"Mice never eat mushrooms or nutty ice cream." The sillier the sentence, the more likely you are to remember it!

Record Breaker

A Japanese man named Akira Haraguchi set a world record for remembering a string of digits in 2006. By using mnemonics he recited 100,000 digits in a mathematical number called pi! This is a number that begins 3.141, but after that the digits go on and on forever, without end. It is called an infinite number. Not many people could train their brain to perform that extraordinary skill, but we can all learn from Akira's technique!

INSIDE YOUR BRAIN

When they are trying to remember a sequence of objects or words, some people make up a story in their head using each item in turn. As they remember the story, they recall the objects or words as well. This works because, when you invent the story, your imagination is creating images in your brain, an extra level of information to help you remember the sequence.

CLOUD

DOG

ORANGUTAN

LOVE

RAINDROP

UNUSUAL

PIGGYBACK

SNAPPY

ALTHOUGH

RUNNING

Study these 10 words for 30 seconds, then close the book. Wait for 1 minute, then see how many you can remember. Now do the same exercise but try to connect the words in a story. Does that help you remember them better?

CHAPTER 3

LONG-TERM MEMORY

Our brains are bombarded with information all day. Most of it will quickly be forgotten unless we make a conscious effort to retain it. That means storing it in our long-term memory. This absolutely amazing "place" is where most of our memories reside. It is not one single spot. We cannot point to our head and say our long-term memory is just there. Instead, our brain has evolved to create the most extraordinary memory system of any creature on Earth.

Our long-term memory has a much, much greater capacity than our short-term memory. In fact, scientists think it can store an unlimited amount of information, for as long as we live. If we sometimes become a little forgetful as we get older, it is not that the information has been lost from our memory, it is that we have some trouble retrieving it successfully. The memory of everything we have ever done and everything we have ever learned is still there, somewhere in the pathways of our brain.

Very young children use their unconscious brain to learn a second language and store it in their long-term memory.

How do we send information to the long-term memory? Scientists think that things we see, hear, and learn are transferred from the short-term memory to the long-term one through a horseshoe-shaped area deep in the brain called the hippocampus. From there, different kinds of information are stored in different areas across the brain.

Conscious and Unconscious Memory

There are two main kinds of long-term memory. The first relates to facts, such as information we have learned and events we remember, such as the two-times table or an amazing birthday party. This is also sometimes called our conscious memory. The second relates to skills and abilities that we develop through life, such as being able to speak, or ride a bike. We learn these things through practice, until we can do them without trying very hard. This is called our unconscious memory.

When we learn a new skill, we use our conscious brain to record it in our long-term memory.

SPEAK YOUR MIND

Have you ever wondered why very young children can learn to speak two languages so easily? They use their unconscious brain to pick up the skill, through listening to people around them speak both languages. Older children and adults, however, have to use their conscious brain to memorize the rules and vocabulary of a new language when they learn it. Do you think people who learn a second language when they are very young also find it easier to learn languages when they are older? Give reasons for your answer.

Facts and Events

You could say that it is our conscious memory that makes us brainy! We can tell other people about all the information we hold in there. Scientists think the temporal lobes are where a lot of these memories are stored. Within our conscious memory, there are actually two different kinds of memory. The first is "knowledge" memories, such as the meaning of words, and facts about the world that we learn in school. We share a lot of these memories with

We learn knowledge of facts and events, such as the Civil War or geography, using one part of our conscious memory.

INSIDE YOUR BRAIN

Have you ever tried to remember
a word and found you just couldn't quite
get it? It feels as if it's "on the tip of your tongue."
Scientists think this may happen because we
learned the word and stored it in our memory in
two different ways. We learned the meaning of
the word but we also learned it by its sound
when it is spoken. When we almost
remember it, and it's "on the tip of our
tongue," we have a clearer memory of
its sound than of its meaning.

other people. Anyone
who has been to
school will know many
of the same things as you.
You may be learning about
the Civil War this year. The kids
in the year above you learned about
it last year, and the kids in the year below will
learn it next year. You will all share that knowledge
when you leave school.

The second kind of conscious memory is quite different. These are
"event" memories, things that have happened to us through our lives.
The wonderful thing is that these are the kinds of memories that make each
one of us unique! No one else's experience of the world will be the same
as yours. Even if they were with you when the memories were made, they
experienced the event differently than you. This is because these memories
include our emotions, how we feel at the time. When we remember a
birthday party from the past, for example, we remember not only who was
there but also how happy or nervous we felt about being invited, or how
much we hoped to win a prize in the games.

How Far Back?

How far back is your earliest memory? The further back you go, the hazier your memories probably become. Have you ever wondered why you cannot remember being a baby, or the day when you took your first steps? Our brains are taking in information from the day we are born, so why do we not have memories from day one?

In fact, part of your memory does actually store and recall things from the very start of your life. Your unconscious memory is working away, learning and storing those skills like speaking and walking. It is your conscious memory that does not stretch that far back. Very few people can remember events from their lives before they were about three years old, and once you are grown up you will not remember much from before you were about seven.

Remember It!

We all need to be able to remember information in our conscious memory. It might be a list of groceries we need for shopping, a group of tasks to complete at work, or knowledge that we will be tested on in school. How easy do you find it to learn and remember information for a test? Do you have a particular way of learning that helps it stick in your memory?

Interestingly, we do have different ways that we prefer to learn. You have probably figured out yours by now. Some people

Very few people can remember anything from the first three years of their life, like taking their first steps. That is a shame as it must have been lots of fun!

If you find out which styles of learning work best for you, it may make schoolwork easier.

learn best by visualizing: by seeing information in charts, pictures, and diagrams. They usually like to write things down, too, so they can read them again. Others prefer to learn by listening to someone talk to them about the subject, and by talking about it themselves. A third group learns best through activity, such as making models or using props to explain something. All three learning styles are equally effective at getting that information into your memory. The key thing is to find the one that works for you.

SPEAK YOUR MIND

Scientists think that one of the reasons we cannot recall events from our first years is that, during those early days, we have not developed the ability to create a "story" out of what happens to us. We do not link the events into a narrative that is memorable. So "I went outside," "I fell down," and "I cuddled with Mom" are not connected into a story. However, "I went outside but fell on the path and hurt myself, so Mom cuddled me and I felt better" is part of a narrative. Do you think that our ability to store memories could be linked to our ability to express ourselves in language? Give reasons for your answer.

Playing Tricks

Our memory is really valuable—we need it to do just about everything. Most of the time it does a great job of keeping us going and getting us to where we need to be. Sometimes, however, it seems to play tricks on us. It's when that happens that we realize just how complex it is, and how much we should appreciate it!

Have you ever had the thought, suddenly and from nowhere, that what is happening has happened before? This doesn't mean yet another spelling test in class, or your mom asking you again to tidy your room. This is different. It feels, for an instant, as if you have been in that exact same situation before, but you cannot quite remember it. This strange feeing is called "déjà vu," which is a French expression meaning "already seen." Exactly what is going on when this happens is unclear, but scientists think it involves the brain's system for checking memories. We may experience déjà vu when the system detects an error between what feels familiar and what we have actually experienced.

Does it ever feel as if you have experienced exactly the same moment before? That feeling is called déjà vu.

Another similar trick our memory can play is "jamais vu." This French expression means "never seen," because this time something that is familiar suddenly becomes strange to us. The best example of this is where you repeat a word over and over, until it seems to lose its meaning and just becomes a weird sound. Try saying the word "shirt" 30 times quickly, and you will be amazed at how it just ends up seeming to have no meaning.

INSIDE YOUR BRAIN

What is happening in the brain when jamais vu occurs? When we say the word, the neurons in the pathways that tell us what it means start to fire. As we say the word again and again, those neurons get so overstimulated they have to stop firing entirely. At that point, we do not recognize the word any longer, and it seems to have no meaning. After a while, the neurons recover and can fire normally again when we say the word.

Jamais vu is a weird feeling that puts your brain in a spin. It is caused by your neurons firing so hard they get overstimulated.

21

CHAPTER 4
MEMORY FOR LIFE

Memory is one of the most powerful and wonderful things that we have. Our conscious memory is what makes us intelligent and successful beings. It allows us to develop skills to an amazing level, to learn, and to communicate what we have learned with each other. If we are lucky, our memory will see us through life from the beginning to the end.

As well as our memory for information and skills, however, we have our memory for experiences. Our memories of good experiences are some of the most precious things we have. They may include those days on the beach with your family, that time your friend made you laugh until you cried, or that day you

Happy times—like the day you got a puppy!—are stored as great memories that we can recall any time we want, to give us pleasure.

finally got the puppy you wanted. We build up a store of these great memories through our life. They shape who we are and give richness to our life. It is wonderful to share a happy memory with someone who was there, or to tell someone else about it.

Troubled Memory

Of course, sometimes our memories are not so good. Sad or scary things happen to everyone, and we learn how to deal with these challenges as we grow up. We learn that when bad things happen, we should think about them, maybe learn something from them, and then move on with our lives. Occasionally, some people have really distressing experiences that have a more lasting effect than normal, everyday troubles. Soldiers in war, for example, can experience great violence and fear. The memory of these bad experiences can cause problems if the sufferers do not have a chance to think through what happened and get past it. Post-traumatic stress disorder (PTSD) is a condition in which harmful memories make it difficult for the sufferer to function in normal life. With the right help, they can recover.

SPEAK YOUR MIND

PTSD is an extreme condition caused by harmful memories, but it is quite common for people with troubling memories to suffer from depression. Once they are given the help they need, to talk about those memories and realize they are in the past and cannot harm them anymore, they can recover. If a friend seems down a lot of the time, you could try starting a conversation about their worries. Talking about our bad memories is often a good way to deal with them. Why do you think this is helpful? Give reasons for your answer.

The scent of a soap can trigger powerful memories from long ago in our childhood.

Memory and Smell

Have you ever walked into a room, sniffed the air, and found yourself suddenly remembering a place or an experience from your past? What is more, the feelings we had in that past time can come back to us, too. It is amazing how often this happens, and how powerful the experience can be, but how can a smell from somewhere today take us back to another place, far away and long ago?

The longer we live, the more likely we are to have memory experiences like this. You may have heard a grandparent or an older friend say that the scent of a particular soap or flower triggers memories from their earlier life. The triggers can be quite unexpected and ordinary, perhaps a cleaning product that was used somewhere memorable in the past. Whatever the trigger, the link is clear, so what is going on in our brain when this happens?

Scientists think the reason is that the area of the brain that processes smell is close to two other important brain areas. First is the hippocampus, the "memory gateway" where things pass through from your short-term to your long-term memory. Second is the amygdala, an area deep in the brain that deals with emotions. So when your brain receives the smell signal from the flower, these neighboring areas can be activated at the same time. Memories in the long-term brain and emotions from the amygdala all come together in your head, leaving you amazed—and confused!

INSIDE YOUR BRAIN

The amygdala is the area of the brain that controls your emotions. It is located deep in the center of the brain, and it deals with basic feelings such as fear. That is an important one, because being afraid of danger is essential to keep us safe and alive! The hippocampus plays a part in our emotional responses, too. It is shaped like a horseshoe and lies deep in the temporal lobe. We also use it to remember the locations of things.

The horseshoe-shaped hippocampus (left) is the "memory gateway." It is very close to the amygdala (right), which deals with basic emotions.

Can We Change Our Brain?

This amazing powerhouse of the brain is with us throughout our life, keeping us alive and making life full of interest and richness, but does it change as the years go by? Also, is it possible for our behavior to affect the structure of our brain and how our memory works?

Scientists think that we start to lay down memories even before we are born. After birth, our brains really get to work. The neurons start to make more and more connections, build more and more networks, and lay down new pathways, as we learn more about the world around us. As we have seen, we cannot remember much at all from the first few years of our lives, but the memories we lay down are still important for our sense of well-being.

In teenage brains, the unused pathways get pruned away, but the ones you do need get faster and more efficient.

INSIDE YOUR BRAIN

Studies have shown that using a particular part of the brain over and over can actually make it change shape. Before GPS was widely used in cars, taxi drivers had to learn the street plan of their city by heart, so that they knew the best route to get from any one place to another. This very particular kind of learning actually made the hippocampus in their brains grow larger. The hippocampus helps us with the location of things, which is what cab drivers become really expert at.

Taxi drivers who learn complex routes around cities can develop a bigger hippocampus.

Study Makes You Strong!

When we become teenagers, changes start to happen in the brain. This is a time when we are studying really hard, taking in lots of factual information so that we can pass exams. This is also the time when our brains start to become more efficient. The pathways that are not used very much are "pruned" away, leaving the ones we do use. This makes us better at the things we need or choose to do. That's why it is a good idea to study hard, and to learn new skills! The things you learn in your teenage years are likely to stay in your memory for many years.

So this means we can change our brains, at least in some ways. By working hard at something, we encourage strong pathways in the brain to form, which in turn makes us better at performing that task. Just as exercising your body makes it stronger, by stretching your muscles and giving your heart and lungs a workout, so it's the same with your brain. This ability of the brain to change with use is called neuroplasticity.

CHAPTER 5

MEMORY HEALTH

The brain is the most complex organ in the body, and understanding how it works is a real challenge. Like every other part of the body, it can develop problems. Parts of it can stop working properly, and cause people difficulty with many aspects of their life, including their memory.

Neurosurgeons carry out complex operations on the brain when it becomes damaged.

It is particularly challenging to study and understand the causes of brain diseases, because we cannot look deep inside a healthy, living brain. We have scanners to take pictures of the inside of the brain, however, and these can tell us a lot about which areas are wasting away, or not "firing" properly. There are surgeons, too, who specialize in operating on the brain. They are called neurosurgeons, and they can perform incredibly intricate operations to repair damage in the outer areas of the brain that can be reached without damaging the rest of it.

Memory Under Stress

There are many things that can affect the health of our memory. If we are feeling very stressed, we can find it more difficult to remember things. The same can be true if we are suffering from a low mood: We just cannot seem to summon up memories in the way we can when we feel okay. A severe blow to the head can also damage our memory. Sometimes the damage will repair itself over time, but in other cases the problems are permanent. This is why it is important to wear a helmet when cycling or skateboarding, or during any other activity where a fall could damage your head.

Getting enough sleep is really important for the health of your brain and memory.

INSIDE YOUR BRAIN

Scientists think that sleep is very important for keeping our memory healthy. When we sleep, our bodies are resting and our brain activity slows right down, too, because we are not taking in new information. This is the time for the brain to catch up on processing everything that came in during the day. New connections are made, and information is stored as memories in the right areas.

Memory Loss

We can all be a bit forgetful sometimes: We don't recall where we left our bag, we leave home without our sports gear, or we cannot remember that information we need for a test. This is normal, but true loss of memory is something else. Memory loss is called amnesia. There are many different kinds of amnesia, and they relate to damage in different parts of the brain.

Back in 1953, Henry Molaison had surgery on his brain to cure a disease called epilepsy that was causing him to have seizures, or fits. The surgeons removed the hippocampus from his brain. After the surgery, his epilepsy was much better, but the effect on his memory was remarkable. Henry could still remember things in his short-term memory, and he could still remember things from his long-term memory, but he could no longer transfer new things from his short- to his long-term memory. Each time he saw a person was like the first time, even his wife. He simply could not remember he had ever seen them before. This taught scientists a lot about the brain, and the important role of the hippocampus in the storing of memories.

It is normal to be a bit forgetful and lose things sometimes.

One particular kind of memory disorder is called prosopagnosia, or face blindness. People with it cannot recognize other people's faces, even the people closest to them that they see all the time. Some people are born with it, while others develop it after a brain injury.

The kind of amnesia where we forget facts and events, in our conscious memory, is more usual than the kind where we forget skills and habits, in our unconscious memory. From our conscious memory, we are more likely to forget more recent memories than ones from long ago. When people with amnesia start to remember things again, older memories come back first, and recent memories last.

Human faces are wonderfully varied, but some people are unable to recognize even their loved ones.

SPEAK YOUR MIND

Most people have a good memory for faces, and we look at faces first to recognize the people we know. If you had prosopagnosia, or face blindness, what other aspects of a person could you use to identify them? Think about your family members, and identify one aspect you could use for each person. Give reasons for your answers.

Dyslexia

Dyslexia is the name given to a learning disability that many children and adults experience. There are different forms of dyslexia, but most people with dyslexia have difficulty with recognizing words, and with writing and spelling them. This affects their literacy learning, but it does not mean they understand less, or are less intelligent. Students with dyslexia are often very smart. Scientists think that the problem they have with words is explained by what is happening in their brain.

Dyslexia affects the way that information is processed, stored in the memory, and retrieved. When learning to read, students with dyslexia have trouble connecting letters to sounds. If you know what the letters "c," "a," and "t" sound like, you can put those sounds together as you read them and say "cat." When we learn to read we need to have a good working memory. This is the short-term memory that allows us to hold information in our head for a short time, as when you hold the beginning of a sentence in your head while you read to the end. In learning to read, we match each letter to its sound and hold that information in our working memory, so we can put them all together to read the word. Dyslexics have a poor working memory for sounds, so they struggle to hold all the letter sounds in their head. This poor working memory for sounds can also make it difficult for people with dyslexia to remember and follow a series of instructions that they are told by a teacher.

Experts have created techniques to help people with dyslexia to improve their working memory. These often include memory games that are performed over and over, to strengthen the pathways in the working memory part of the brain. The results of tests show that these can really help with reading. The great thing is that it helps with all other areas of learning too, as an improved working memory also gives students better concentration, and more confidence.

SPEAK YOUR MIND

Can you imagine how difficult it must be if you have dyslexia and find reading and other forms of learning more difficult? Your working memory may be faulty, but that does not mean you are less smart than everyone else. How do you think people learning alongside dyslexics can help and support them? Give reasons for your answer.

Having dyslexia need not stop you from achieving your goals. Many successful people, such as movie director Steven Spielberg, are dyslexic.

People who have had a stroke can get help with rehabilitation from physical therapists.

Brain Attack

Sometimes things go seriously wrong in the brain. A stroke is a serious medical event, when the blood supply to part of the brain is stopped. This can be because a blood vessel is blocked, or when one bursts open and blood leaks out. When this happens, the brain cells in the affected area die because they are not getting the oxygen they need from the blood. The area of the brain where this happens cannot work properly. This brain damage affects many different areas of the body, and it often affects the memory, too.

Strokes most commonly happen to older people. The most common effects of a stroke are the inability to move arms and legs on one side of the body, to speak properly, and to see things on one side. If the brain's temporal lobe has been affected by a stroke, the person's memory is likely to be damaged. They find it especially difficult to remember new information, and to concentrate.

If the stroke is not too severe, many of its effects will improve over time. This recovery period can range from a few weeks to over a year. Patients are given therapy to improve their movement, and as the brain gradually repairs itself many of the damaged functions will get better, though they are unlikely to return to how they were originally. The memory problems can improve, too, although unfortunately people who have had a stroke that affected their memory are more likely to develop other brain health problems in the future.

Talking about memories with an elderly person who has had a stroke can help them recover.

INSIDE YOUR BRAIN

Strokes happen suddenly, so they are very hard to predict, but a person having a stroke will show some or all of these signs: dizziness, a very bad headache, loss of balance, inability to raise both arms above their head, slurred speech, and a numbness on one side of their face. If they show these signs, they must get to the hospital right away.

CHAPTER 6

THE AGING BRAIN

For most people, our super-brains allow us to live a full life for many, many years. Our experiences change as we grow up, but still the brain stores them all away in our long-term memory. We get even better at the skills we learned when we were young, and we learn new ones to store in our unconscious memory. As with all the processes in our body, however, as we get older our memory can suffer from the effects of aging.

As we get older, we should keep our brain challenged with activities that make us think.

Our brain processing power and memory for detail peaks at about age 18. But that does not mean that we are past it from then on, that our brains are declining altogether! In fact, there are several memory-related skills that we get better at over several decades. Our ability to recognize and identify faces peaks in our 30s. Amazingly, our concentration skills peak in our 40s, when we are best at staying focused on a task. You might think that our ability to do basic math peaks in school, but scientists have found that we are best at math at around age 50. At every stage of life, up to about age 70, we are at our best in some things, even if other skills are starting to decline.

Age Creeps In

Once we reach old age, however, changes do begin to show. Interestingly, our memory for facts and information remains good for longer than our memory for experiences. So we are more likely to remember our times tables, or details of the history of the nineteenth century, than to remember a conversation we had with a friend a few years ago. Scientists think this is because "experience" memories are more complex: When we remember experiences, we have to recall the whole context in which they happened. So, for example, for that conversation with a friend you recall not only what you said but where you were and the reason you were together.

INSIDE YOUR BRAIN

Tests show that our peak for vocabulary skills is when we are in our late 60s, which may sound surprising. After more than six decades of life, we have had time to store a huge number of words in our memory, to understand their meaning, and to enrich our lives by using them regularly. The pathways in the brain have not yet started to break down enough for us to lose this store of treasure.

We can learn new skills, and keep up with new technology, at any age.

Exercising with friends is great for keeping your brain healthy.

Use It or Lose It

Your amazing brain likes being used! The billions of neurons that are frantically making trillions of connections all the time, strengthening the pathways across your brain and storing up millions of memories, need something to work on. While you are awake, you should keep lively!

There are lots of things we can do to keep our brains in good shape. The first thing is true for the whole body, and that's to exercise regularly. Being physically fit and giving the heart and lungs a good workout helps keep the brain supplied with all the oxygen-rich blood that it needs. Your brain is a hungry organ! It uses one-fifth of all the energy you consume. People who keep fit through their life and into old age often suffer less memory loss. A healthy diet is just as important for brain health. Eating lots of fresh fruit, vegetables, and whole grains, as well as oily fish such as salmon and tuna, will give you the nutrients you need. Avoid fatty and sugary foods, which are not brain-friendly.

At school you are using your brain every day, but as we get older some people find they become less mentally active. Keep your mind busy by playing games and puzzles, especially ones that push you and make you think a bit harder. Doing this with other people is good for you, too, as being sociable and hanging out with friends keeps the brain and the memory switched on.

Sleep Well

As well as being active, your brain also desperately needs down time. You should get at least eight hours of sleep at night, probably more when you're a teenager. When we sleep the brain does maintenance on the pathways and storage of memories. When we lack sleep, we become more stressed and our mood can suffer. This isn't good for our memory.

SPEAK YOUR MIND

Tests have shown that we find it easier to store memories when we are concentrating. We spend lots of time multitasking, especially with technology all around us, but it's easier to learn and remember things if your attention is not divided. Think about how you do homework. Are you distracted by a cell phone or music? What distraction affects you the most, and why? Give reasons for your answer.

We learn most effectively when we are concentrating on just one source of information, so put away the phone and turn off the music when you are working!

Dementia sufferers may forget the names of everyday objects.

Dementia

As old age progresses, it is normal for the brain to lose some of its processing power. Everything takes a little longer, including recalling memories and completing tasks. Sometimes, however, some older people suffer more than a normal level of impaired memory. Their ability to think and to remember breaks down so far that they find it difficult to function in everyday life. This is called dementia.

Dementia becomes more common as people get older. About 5 percent of people aged 65 have dementia, and by the age of 85–90 about 50 percent of people have it. People with dementia forget the names of everyday things, and may not recognize people close to them. As their dementia gets worse, they lose the ability to look after themselves. Sadly, we do not have a cure for dementia, but there are some drugs that can slow down its progress, and scientists are working very hard to find better treatments.

The best-known and most common type of dementia is Alzheimer's disease, which accounts for 50–70 percent of all dementia cases. It is caused when the neurons in some areas of the brain start to die and the connections are lost. People with Alzheimer's lose the ability to make new memories, and to remember events from their past. They can also suffer from mood swings and become irritable and aggressive. The second most common type of dementia is called vascular dementia. This is caused by damage to the brain during a stroke. The blood supply is cut off, by either a clot in a blood vessel or a burst blood vessel. The symptoms are similar to those of Alzheimer's disease.

INSIDE YOUR BRAIN

The best way to find out if someone is suffering from dementia is to do a scan of their brain. A magnetic resonance imaging (MRI) scan creates a detailed picture of the inside of the brain. This shows any areas where the brain is degenerating. The brains of dementia patients deteriorate in the hippocampus, the temporal lobes, the parietal lobe, and parts of the frontal lobe.

These MRI scans of a healthy brain (left) and the brain of a person with dementia (right) show the damage caused by dementia. The red and yellow areas are active.

The Best Brains in Action

Humans have been wondering for thousands of years how we have these amazing powers to think and remember. One famous ancient Greek thinker named Aristotle believed that our emotions were all controlled by our heart! Gradually, over the centuries, we have realized that the brain is pretty important in controlling everything we do and feel. Scientists have been working hard to get to the bottom of this ingenious, large lump of gray matter, to figure out exactly what it can do, and how it does it.

Today, science is working harder than ever before to unlock the secrets of the brain. We have great technology that can help us do this, such as scanners that can show us what is going on deep inside the brain. We now have a pretty good brain map, showing which areas are responsible for which kinds of activity. We also have powerful microscopes that can show us exactly what neurons look like, and how they connect with each other to send trillions of electric signals across the brain.

Our knowledge of the brain has progressed enormously, but there is still much more to learn.

The longest nerve in the body is the vagus nerve. It connects the brain to the stomach and other organs.

There is still so much more to find out, however. The brain is definitely the "new frontier" of the human body. The study of the brain is called neuroscience, and there are tens of thousands of scientists around the world today working to unlock the brain's secrets. One of the most urgent answers needed is a cure for dementia, because it affects so many people. It is difficult to test new drugs on living people, but scientists recently managed to reproduce human brain cells in the laboratory. This is really exciting, because now scientists can use these cells to test a wide range of possible drug treatments, and examine them to learn more about how the disease develops in patients.

Another breakthrough area of research is the link between having a healthy brain and a healthy gut! Amazingly, scientists think that the number of "good" bacteria we have in our digestive system may affect how our brain works, and how diseases develop.

SPEAK YOUR MIND

It may seem weird that your gut health and brain health might be connected, but the two are physically connected by a long nerve, called the vagus nerve, so maybe it's not so surprising. Do you think this shows the importance of keeping an open mind when searching for new areas of scientific research? Give reasons for your answer.

AMAZING MEMORY

We have seen that the most powerful and extraordinary organ in the human body still holds many mysteries for us. It acts like a computer, controlling everything we do, but unlike any computer we have ever built, it is constantly rewiring itself as it learns new things. Somewhere across its network of neurons is stored everything we have ever done and all we know.

Your memory is what keeps you going. Your unconscious memory tells you how to walk, to speak, and do a thousand different tasks, every minute of the day.

When you score a goal, you build a great new memory!

INSIDE YOUR BRAIN

Neuroscientists think of the brain as a network of connected circuits, made up of billions of neurons. To understand it, they need to study different areas of science, including math and computers, biology and medicine. It's like a puzzle, one of the greatest puzzles on Earth. How can we solve the mystery of brainpower? By putting the considerable power of our impressive brains together!

Your conscious memory allows you to soak up knowledge like a sponge, to pass tests, and to follow your interests so you can get great at the things you enjoy. It also allows you to remember many experiences that happen every day. All the wonderful things that happen, and the not so good as well, build up into a rich collection of memories that will last you a lifetime, and shape who you are.

Somehow, the feelings we get when we spend time with someone we love, or the feelings of achieving something we have wanted for a long time, are translated into electrical signals inside our brains. These signals whiz around the network and are stored away as memories. That does sound rather like magic, but scientists are getting closer all the time to unlocking the secrets of how it happens.

GLOSSARY

Alzheimer's A disease of the brain that makes people forgetful.

amnesia Loss of memory.

amygdala The area of the brain that deals with emotions.

axon A long tentacle that extends from a neuron to send signals to other neurons.

brain stem The part of the base of the brain that controls our heartbeat and breathing.

cerebellum The area at the back of the brain that controls the working of our muscles.

cerebral cortex The outside layer of the brain that is deeply folded and used for many key functions.

dementia A range of conditions where a person loses a significant amount of their memory.

dendrite A shorter tentacle that extends from a neuron to receive signals from other neurons.

depression A condition in which a person suffers from a low mood over a long period.

dyslexia A learning disability that causes difficulty with literacy.

hemisphere One of the two halves of the brain.

hippocampus A horseshoe-shaped area in the inner brain thought to be a "gateway" between the short-term and long-term memory.

lobe A curved or rounded part of something. Each hemisphere of the brain is divided into four lobes: frontal, parietal, occipital, and temporal.

long-term memory The brain's capacity to hold and process information for a long time.

magnetic resonance imaging (MRI) scan A process in which a scanning machine takes detailed pictures of the inside of the body.

mnemonic A phrase used to help us remember something.

neuron A nerve cell.

neuroscience The study of the brain and the nervous system.

nutrients The substances in foods that we need to eat to keep healthy.

post-traumatic stress disorder (PTSD) A severe condition caused by horrible experiences and memories.

sensory memory The very short-term memories that are formed from information from our senses such as sight, hearing, and smell.

short-term memory The brain's capacity to hold and process information for a short time.

FOR MORE INFORMATION

Books

Abramovitz, Melissa. *Brain Science*. Minneapolis, MN: Essential Library, 2016.

Haseltine, Eric. *Brain Safari: 5-Minute Experiments to Explore the Space Between Your Ears*. Austin, TX: Greenleaf Book Group, 2018.

Meister, Cari. *Totally Wacky Facts About the Mind*. North Mankato, MN: Capstone Press, 2016.

Swanson, Jennifer. *Brain Games: The Mind-Blowing Science of Your Amazing Brain*. Washington, DC: National Geographic Kids, 2015.

Websites

Find out more about memory and what affects it at:
brainmadesimple.com/memory

Discover the different parts of the brain at:
ducksters.com/science/brain.php

Read plenty more about the brain at:
easyscienceforkids.com/all-about-your-amazing-brain

Learn more about memory and the brain at:
kidshealth.org/en/kids/memory.html

INDEX